Being Brave

by Jill Lynn Donahue   illustrated by Stacey Previn

PICTURE WINDOW BOOKS
Minneapolis, Minnesota

Special thanks to our advisers for their expertise:

Kay Augustine
National Director and Character Education Specialist, Ignite
West Des Moines, Iowa

Terry Flaherty, Ph.D., Professor of English
Minnesota State University, Mankato

Editor: Shelly Lyons
Designer: Tracy Davies
Page Production: Melissa Kes
Art Director: Nathan Gassman
Associate Managing Editor: Christianne Jones
The illustrations in this book were created with acrylics.

Picture Window Books
5115 Excelsior Boulevard
Suite 232
Minneapolis, MN 55416
877-845-8392
www.picturewindowbooks.com

Printed in the United States of America.

 All books published by Picture Window Books
are manufactured with paper containing at least
10 percent post-consumer waste.

Library of Congress Cataloging-in-Publication Data
Donahue, Jill L. (Jill Lynn), 1967-
Being brave / by Jill Lynn Donahue ; illustrated by
Stacey Previn.
p. cm. – (Way to be!)
Includes bibliographical references and index.
ISBN-13: 978-1-4048-3780-5 (library binding)
ISBN-10: 1-4048-3780-9 (library binding)
1. Courage–Juvenile literature. I. Previn, Stacey. II. Title.
BJ1533.C8D655 2008
179'.6–dc22   2007004571

Being brave means facing your fears. Brave people do the right thing, even when it is not easy. Brave people may feel afraid sometimes. But they do what needs to be done. There are many ways to be brave.

The doctor says Alexa needs two shots. Alexa doesn't like shots, but she knows they will keep her healthy.

Alexa is being brave.

Cass and Danny are afraid of spiders. Cass catches a spider in a cup and takes it outdoors.

Cass is being brave.

Eddie's friends think it is cool to take off their hats while waiting for the bus. Eddie knows his friends might tease him, but he leaves his hat on.

Eddie is being brave.

Anna and Joy don't like eating fish. But at the world food fair, Anna tries sushi.

Anna is being brave.

Tim is worried about his first trip on an airplane. But he holds his mom's hand and gets on the plane.

Tim is being brave.

13

Ben wants to ride the roller coaster with Tyrone. Even though Tyrone is afraid, he decides to try it.

Tyrone is being brave.

Enrico doesn't like talking in front of his class. He takes a deep breath and tells a funny story.

Enrico is being brave.

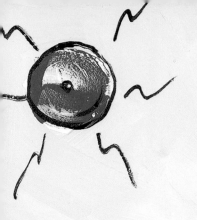

The fire alarm goes off at school. The students listen to their teacher and quickly leave the building.

The students are being brave.

19

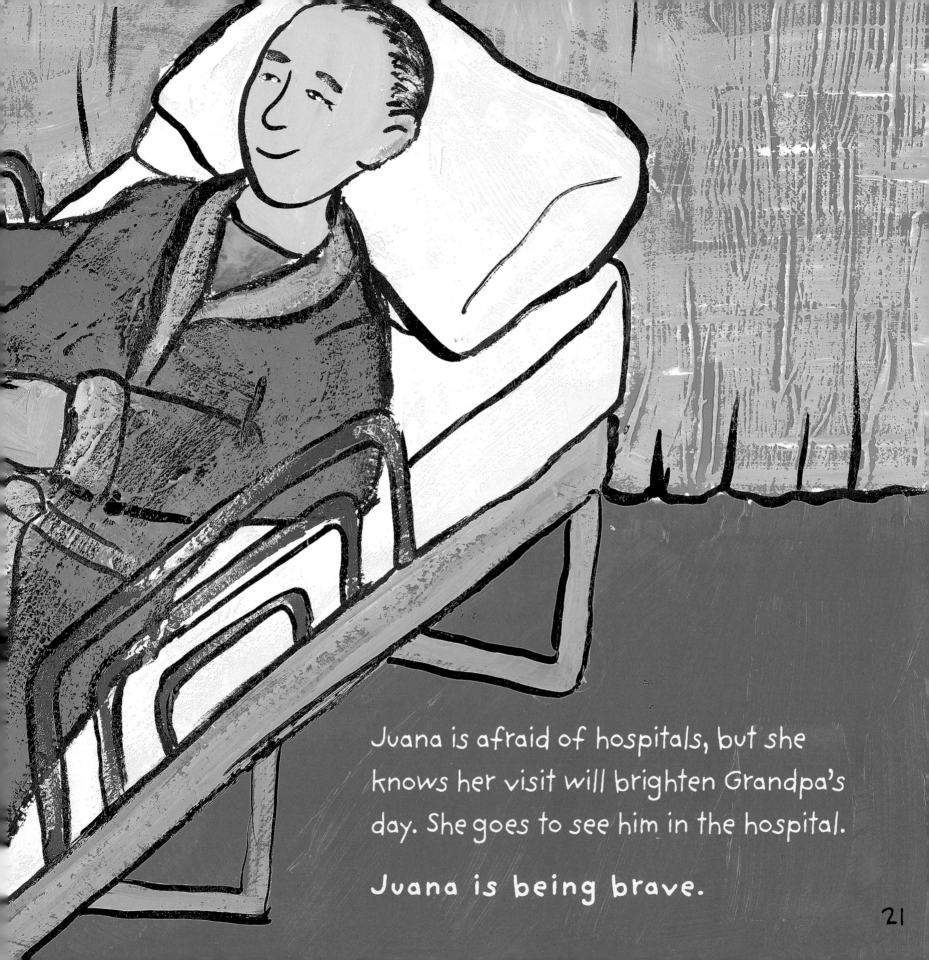

Juana is afraid of hospitals, but she knows her visit will brighten Grandpa's day. She goes to see him in the hospital.

Juana is being brave.

21

Hannah has never been to the dentist and is scared that it will hurt. She sits still while the dentist does his work.

Hannah is being brave.

To Learn More

At the Library

Crum, Shutta. *The Bravest of the Brave.* New York: Alfred A. Knopf, 2005.
Finn, Carrie. *Kids Talk About Bravery.* Minneapolis: Picture Window Books, 2006.
Stein, Mathilde. *Brave Ben.* Asheville, N.C.: Front Street, 2006.

On the Web

FactHound offers a safe, fun way to find Web sites related to this book.
All of the sites on FactHound have been researched by our staff.

1. Visit www.facthound.com
2. Type in this special code: 1404837809
3. Click on the FETCH IT button.

Your trusty FactHound will fetch the best sites for you!

Index

Look for all of the books in the Way to Be! series: